AF228222

Artificial Intelligence in the Workplace

Will AI Help Us or Hurt Us?

Nick Hunter

CHERITON
CHILDREN'S BOOKS

Published in 2025 by **Cheriton Children's Books**
1 Bank Drive West, Shrewsbury, Shropshire, SY3 9DJ, UK

© 2025 Cheriton Children's Books

First Edition

Author: Nick Hunter
Designers: Paul Myerscough and Jessica Moon
Editor: Sarah Eason
Proofreader: Kate Hobson

Picture credits: Cover: Shutterstock/Ground Picture (foreground), Shutterstock/Gorodenkoff (background); Inside: Throughout: Shutterstock/Nadya Art, p1: Shutterstock/Industryviews, p5b: Shutterstock/PopTika, p5t: Shutterstock/Redpixel.pl, p6: Shutterstock/Stokkete, p7: Shutterstock/Lenscap Photography, p8: Shutterstock/Industryviews, p9: Shutterstock/Sabisaftoiu, p10: Shutterstock/Ground Picture, p11: Shutterstock/Photoroyalty, p12: Shutterstock/Metamorworks, p13: Shutterstock/Sean Pavone, p14: Shutterstock/Toa55, p15: Shutterstock/CrizzyStudio, p18: Shutterstock/Everett Collection, p19: Shutterstock/TippaPatt, p20: Shutterstock/Thongden Studio, p21: Shutterstock/Josiah True, p22: Shutterstock/vichie81, p23: Shutterstock/Masarik, p24: Shutterstock/Stokkete, p25: Shutterstock/Monkey Business Images, p29: Shutterstock/Igor Link, p30: Shutterstock/Rangizzz, p31: Shutterstock/Gorodenkoff, p34: Shutterstock/Gorodenkoff, p35: Shutterstock/Kitreel, p36: Shutterstock/Andrey Popov, p37: Shutterstock/Fizkes, p41: Shutterstock/DC Studio, p44: Shutterstock/G-Stock Studio, p47: Shutterstock/Metamorworks.

Printed in China

Please visit our website,
www.cheritonchildrensbooks.com
to see more of our high-quality books.

Contents

Introduction
What Is Artificial Intelligence? 4

Chapter 1
The History of AI at Work 6

Chapter 2
AI and the Working Day 10

Chapter 3
AI and Jobs 18

Chapter 4
Cybercrime and Security 28

Chapter 5
Are You Ready for AI? 34

Chapter 6
Friend or Foe? 40

Conclusion
The Ethics of AI 44

Find Out More 45

Glossary 46

Index and About the Author 48

What Is Artificial Intelligence?

Artificial intelligence (AI) is already affecting many aspects of business and the workplace. If you contact a big company to inquire or complain about a product, your first contact will be with a **chatbot**, which will ask if you need help or reply to your question. These online assistants are designed to answer our questions just as a human would, using natural language but drawing on large amounts of data to find the most useful answer. The business hopes its happy customers will have any questions answered more efficiently. But if computers can deal with customer questions, what happens to the people who used to do this type of work? AI is rapidly changing the way that we work and our workplaces.

HOW DO WE DEFINE AI?

Before we look at the many changes it could bring to our lives, let's consider what we mean by artificial intelligence. Artificial intelligence describes the way that **software** or machines can be designed and programmed to do things that can normally only be carried out by intelligent beings, including humans. These things could include recognizing human speech, making complex decisions, and carrying out complex tasks based on these decisions.

THINKING MACHINES

As humans, we are constantly processing data to make decisions. If we write an email or message to a company, we need to consider what words we use to communicate our ideas. We know that formal language in a letter or email is very different from the way we would speak to a friend. For a computer to be able to create a formal message, which seems natural to us, complex processes and huge amounts of data are required. However, when computers are able to **replicate** human thoughts and write text or other media that appears to be created by a person, this can have a powerful impact on the world and our place in it.

If AI tools can respond to questions like a human, this means big changes for many industries.

THE BENEFITS AND THE RISKS

Since the beginning of the twenty-first century, there have been huge steps forward in the development of AI. Many people believe that the changes brought about by this technology are only just beginning and will affect all areas of our lives. This will undoubtedly change the way we work, as AI takes on some of the tasks that human workers have done in the past. Some people are concerned that AI will actually replace humans in many jobs, which could change the way we all live our lives. Will this be the case or will there still be a place for humans in the workplace? We'll explore this idea in the book and examine the changes that AI will bring to the way we all work.

This book will look at how AI could change the workplace and **debate** whether this new technology is our friend or **foe**. Look for **IS AI A FRIEND OR FOE?** throughout the book. Read the arguments for and against AI, then answer questions that invite you to draw your own conclusions about whether this transformative technology will help us or hurt us.

CHAPTER 1

The History of AI at Work

AI is not a new idea, and there are many examples of how it already affects the world of work. The term "artificial intelligence" was first used in the 1950s, long before computers became common in most offices. A lot of research into the possibilities of AI took place during the 1960s and 1970s, but the computers of the time were not powerful enough to make great progress in handling the quantities of data needed to make AI possible.

WORKING ONLINE

The invention of the World Wide Web (WWW) and its growth in the 1990s led to dramatic changes in the world of work. It meant that people and businesses around the world could share ideas and information. Companies such as Amazon were quick to grasp the opportunities of selling products online. Computers started to show that they could solve complex problems as well as humans, such as when the Deep Blue computer managed to defeat world champion Garry Kasparov at chess in 1997.

Before the 1970s, many workplaces did not even contain a computer.

A statue of computing **pioneer** Alan Turing.

ORGANIZING DATA

The need to organize and **navigate** all the data on the Web led to the development of search engines such as Google, which was launched in 1998. Search engines use very complex **algorithms** that **predict** which results will be most useful to the searcher, making them an early form of AI. Shopping sites also use similar methods to predict which products we will want to buy. True AI systems use vast amounts of data to train search engines in processing natural language and making **predictions**, and the development of new AI tools could mean a big leap forward in search engines, making it easier than ever to refine searches, plan a vacation, or even prepare for a job interview.

The Turing Test

British scientist Alan Turing was one of the pioneers of computing. Turing proposed a test to decide if a computer or other machine demonstrated AI. Turing said that if a computer acts and reacts like a human being, so we cannot tell the difference between the two, then it is showing true AI. Turing called this test "the Imitation Game."

SPEECH RECOGNITION

The first speech recognition systems began to appear in the late 1990s. Developments in speech recognition enable computers to understand human speech patterns and respond with useful answers. Many of us are familiar with voice-activated assistants at home, such as Amazon's Alexa or Apple's Siri. Speech recognition is one area in which AI is changing many workplaces. Customer calls will often be sorted by **automated** systems that respond to what the caller says, and chatbots are now able to respond to complex questions from customers too.

BIG DATA

With the growth of social media in the early 2000s, everyone could share information about their lives. We now live in an era of "big data." Corporations can collect and use all sorts of information about us, from the websites we visit to the photos we share on social media. This ocean of data is too big and complex for humans to investigate easily, so AI systems have been developed to understand the data. Businesses can use AI to organize this data and make it a powerful tool of the business. For example, social media sites can use what they know about us to attract advertisers and sell us products.

NEW AND OLD JOBS

Many jobs that were common at one time have been replaced by technology. Most bank tellers were replaced by ATMs many years ago. Other jobs such as grocery store checkout and warehouse workers have been replaced more recently. Although many of these jobs have not been replaced by AI technology, it could accelerate this process for many industries. However, changing technology and the development of AI have created many new jobs in computing and data science in which workers try to manage the development of AI and use the technology to change our lives.

GPUs and AI

The huge growth of AI depended on something that was already part of gaming consoles. The graphics processing unit (GPU) is a computer chip that can process a lot of information very quickly. GPUs were first used in gaming because they could handle the high-quality, fast-moving graphics that are part of many games. GPUs became the key **hardware** for AI developers who also wanted to process lots of data at very high speeds for **deep learning**.

When you order something online, it may be collected and processed by a **robot**.

CHAPTER 2

AI and the Working Day

Office life has changed dramatically since the 1980s, when computers started to appear on every desk. AI could drive the next great revolution in the workplace. Office jobs could be particularly affected by the growth of AI as businesses look for AI tools that will make their workers more **productive**.

PERSONAL ASSISTANTS

Most office workers spend much of their time on **routine** tasks such as sending and responding to emails, writing reports, creating marketing copy, and other social media posts. In the future, generative AI will take care of many of these tasks.

Generative AI tools can create a report based on a specific collection of data or deal with many everyday communications, with little input from a human worker. AI assistants could also work together to set up meetings for different people, automatically checking calendars and preparing everything needed.

AI can take over routine tasks such as arranging meetings and taking notes.

AI systems learn all the time, so speech recognition improves as the systems are exposed to different language and voices.

ADDING AI FEATURES

Big technology companies such as Microsoft and Google are adding AI features to their existing office software products. These tech giants hope that their AI solutions will become a part of every office, just as previous products such as Microsoft's Office software and Google's search engine have become regular office features.

USING SPEECH RECOGNITION

Using natural language and speech is one of the most important features of AI for its use in the workplace. This technology could be used for regular office tasks such as scheduling meetings or searching for information. Office workers can also **dictate** messages or letters wherever they are, such as when traveling. We don't always think of this as AI because we are so used to speech recognition on phones or smart speakers, but smooth **transcribing** from voice to written text involves lots of training and data to make it appear natural.

What Is Generative AI?

OpenAI's ChatGPT is an example of a generative AI tool. It is trained on a massive **database** of language from the Internet. Rather than scanning information to identify or **classify** particular data, generative AI uses a prompt, such as a simple question, and creates answers that are similar to what it has been trained on to create reports or even reconstruct pictures in a particular chosen style.

Translating your voice into other languages could help you communicate with people all over the world.

JUST THE FACTS

For professionals such as lawyers, speech recognition can be an especially helpful tool. When lawyers meet with their clients, it is essential that they have accurate notes from these meetings. Just a simple mistake could determine whether a criminal is found guilty or destroy a multi-million dollar deal. The latest speech recognition tools can make sure that notes are accurate and also save time.

FOR EVERYONE

One of the most difficult issues to crack is to make sure speech recognition works equally well for different voices and accents, and also in different languages. The early examples of speech recognition software only worked for a fairly narrow group of people speaking English without a strong accent or any disability. It's no accident that these people were very like the people developing AI solutions for tech companies in the United States and their customers. People who did not fit this group were excluded or disadvantaged by speech recognition systems, such as automated call centers.

AROUND THE WORLD

Companies are now working to expand spoken language to some of the thousands of languages around the world, which could bring huge benefits for communication between speakers of different languages. This will also help with some of the issues that speech recognition software finds most difficult: unusual addresses and names, numbers, and **currencies**.

SELLING PRODUCTS

Generative AI can also create pictures and designs, and this makes it easier for businesses to market and advertise their products.

However, there is always a risk that if everyone uses AI for designing brochures and advertisements, they will all look the same. The whole point of advertising products is to make them stand out from the crowd so they will be easily noticed.

SOLD BY AI

Chatbots are already common in customer service but AI salespeople may not be far away. These **avatars** could explain new and complex products to customers and be able to answer any question the customer has. While this could change sales forever, it is also well known that many customers would be unhappy about talking to a machine, even if all of their questions were answered perfectly. Those customers would prefer to talk directly to a human being.

A TASTY FUTURE

Some companies even boast about how AI has been used to develop their products. One well-known soda company has highlighted how AI has been used to design new flavors that are intended to make soda-lovers think of a "positive future" rather than being named after any particular known flavor. It's not always clear exactly what contribution AI has made to these products but it helps companies present them as a bright and exciting taste of the future.

Companies want their advertisements to stand out from the crowd.

See pages 16-17 for more on the debate about AI and customer service.

Farmers use data all the time to monitor progress of crops and check when they are ready to harvest. Self-driving vehicles would help them make farmwork quicker and easier.

ON THE FARM

There are many ways in which AI will affect office-based service industries. What about a specific and very different type of industry? There are many start-up companies looking at how they could use AI in agriculture for growing our food. Self-driving tractors and combine harvesters are already available, and able to navigate themselves. Compared to self-driving cars, farm vehicles do not have to deal with issues such as crowded roads and avoiding people crossing the street.

AI FARMERS

AI could lead to even smarter vehicles, such as **drones** that monitor crops for pests and weeds, which can then reduce the overall use of **pesticides**. AI systems can also monitor soils and water levels to make sure crops have the best conditions for growth. Farmers hope that AI can make their land more productive and cut the amount of crops that are wasted.

CAUSES FOR CONCERN

Many people are concerned that the AI revolution at work will not be a good thing for everyone. Using the example of agriculture, there will be costs in taking on AI technology to improve productivity. Even in wealthy countries, many farmers may not be able to afford to invest in AI, and this could even lead to farms closing. In developing countries, the gap between farms that can afford AI and the others could be even greater. This pattern could also be true in other areas of industry. The next chapter looks in greater detail at the impact that AI could have on people's jobs.

BIG MISTAKES

Not everyone is sure that AI assistants will have such a big impact on the office. While it can be annoying if your smart speaker doesn't always recognize what you say immediately, errors can cause big problems for businesses. Corporations need to be sure that AI does the right thing every time. Generative AI tools create documents similar to those that already exist, and which may not contain accurate information. Early examples of AI-generated documents have often included content that is not actually true. Businesses need to be sure that this will not happen before they use AI to write important reports.

WHO'S THE BOSS?

Many people are also worried about the effect that use of AI in the workplace could have on workers and customers. All humans need time to relax and downtime away from work. However, if AI is taking on tasks and working constantly, this could increase pressure on workers. Bosses could use AI to monitor their employees for every minute they are at work to ensure they meet targets. Rather than helping us, AI could start taking charge of entire workplaces.

Some people worry that AI errors could cause as many problems as they solve.

AI Will Improve Customer Service

Corporations hope that AI will make their businesses better. They believe that using the technology will help workers be far more efficient and serve customers better. Perhaps AI will improve the customer's experience. There are arguments both for and against this scenario. Let's take a look at them.

AGREE

More efficient systems: AI tools will enable businesses to do things more efficiently, such as processing orders, dealing with questions, and communicating with customers.

More focus on customers: If AI assistants can take over many routine and administrative jobs, this will give people more time to focus on improving how they serve customers and improve services. That will improve the customer's experience.

Better speech recognition: Speech recognition and **natural language processing (NLP)** will make experiences better for customers, who may not even know they're talking to a computer.

A more personal service: AI will be able to use detailed data about customers or other factors to help businesses give a more personal service. A human worker could not achieve the same.

DISAGREE

People like people: We like things to be convenient but many people also like to interact with other people. Will people be happy to use the convenience of AI rather than meeting people when they deal with a business? Will businesses be able to run in this way?

AI helps big business: The growth of AI could benefit the biggest businesses that can afford to invest in new technology and so lead to less choice for customers. Less competition could mean poorer service or higher prices. That would be detrimental to people.

Cutting costs: Will businesses use AI tools as a way to cut costs rather than improve how they work? If AI is used to replace human workers, this could lead to worse experiences for customers.

Conclusion

AI tools will benefit businesses by improving systems and cutting costs, but it is not certain that these changes will benefit customers. This could be especially true if the growth of AI means that there are too few people employed to support customers when they need them.

Q Do you think AI will improve the customer's experience or do you think it will make it worse?

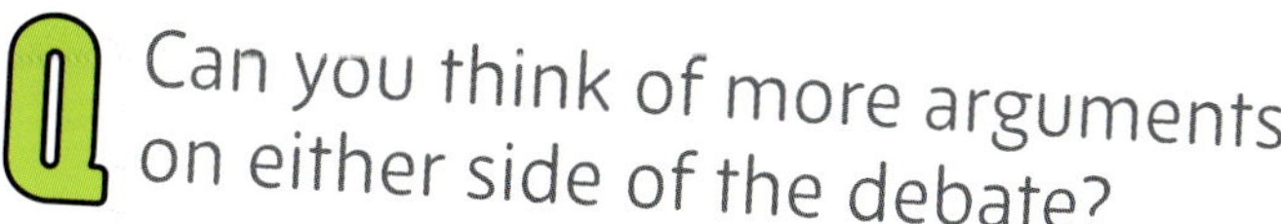

Q Can you think of more arguments on either side of the debate?

Q Will AI be a friend or a foe? What conclusions do you draw?

CHAPTER 3

AI and Jobs

Most people agree that AI tools will be able to do routine tasks more easily and efficiently than humans. But how will this affect the people who currently spend their working lives doing these tasks? It will certainly mean big changes, but also could mean there are fewer jobs for people. In the future, AI may also start to perform tasks that need more specialist skills and knowledge. If that happens, it could mean a major reshaping of how people work and the jobs they do.

POSITIVE CHANGES

AI will bring positive changes to people's working lives. For example, the continuing development of voice-recognition tools can make it much easier to communicate with businesses and other people. Businesses will be able to produce more or serve more customers at lower cost using the AI resources they have. This should benefit us all. However, many people predict that AI will enable businesses to do this while employing fewer people than they have in the past, and this will mean that there are not enough jobs for all those who need them.

Technology has changed the way we work many times in the past, but AI could have an even bigger impact.

Chatbots are already handling many customer service tasks.

BENEFIT FOR EMPLOYERS

Building workplaces that can be controlled and operated by AI tools will require a lot of investment from employers, so what is in it for them? Well, robots and chatbots can work 24 hours a day, 365 days per year. They can perform tasks efficiently without the need for lunch or rest breaks. Chatbots can also deal with many customer queries at once.

FEAR OF CHANGING TECHNOLOGY

People have been warning for hundreds of years about the effect of automation and new technology on people's jobs. This has worried people since the start of the first Industrial Revolution around 1750.

There are predictions that the AI revolution will be very different from major changes in technology that have taken place in the past.

A NEW INDUSTRIAL REVOLUTION

During the Industrial Revolution, more goods were manufactured in factories using machines that could produce things such as textiles and metal goods quicker than individual craftspeople. Two centuries later, the growth of the Internet affected jobs in areas such as **retail** because people bought more goods online and stopped visiting physical stores. So, in both these examples, particular industries were affected. However, the AI revolution could have an even greater impact.

WHERE WILL AI HAVE MOST EFFECT?

Unlike in previous periods of changing technology, the jobs most under threat from AI are "white collar" jobs held by people with a high level of education or college degree. Let's look in more detail at some of the industries likely to be most affected by the march of AI.

CUSTOMER SERVICES

If you visit a retailer's website or try to call your cell phone provider, you are likely already dealing with AI. Most questions customers ask are routine: where is my order, or can I cancel or upgrade my contract? These issues can be most efficiently solved by AI, so companies can employ fewer human operatives. Humans are employed to deal with more complex problems and check how the system is working.

BANKING AND FINANCE

Banks are already using AI to deal with customer requests and to monitor accounts for signs of **fraud** or unusual activity. AI can deal with many complex financial transactions more quickly and efficiently than a human employee.

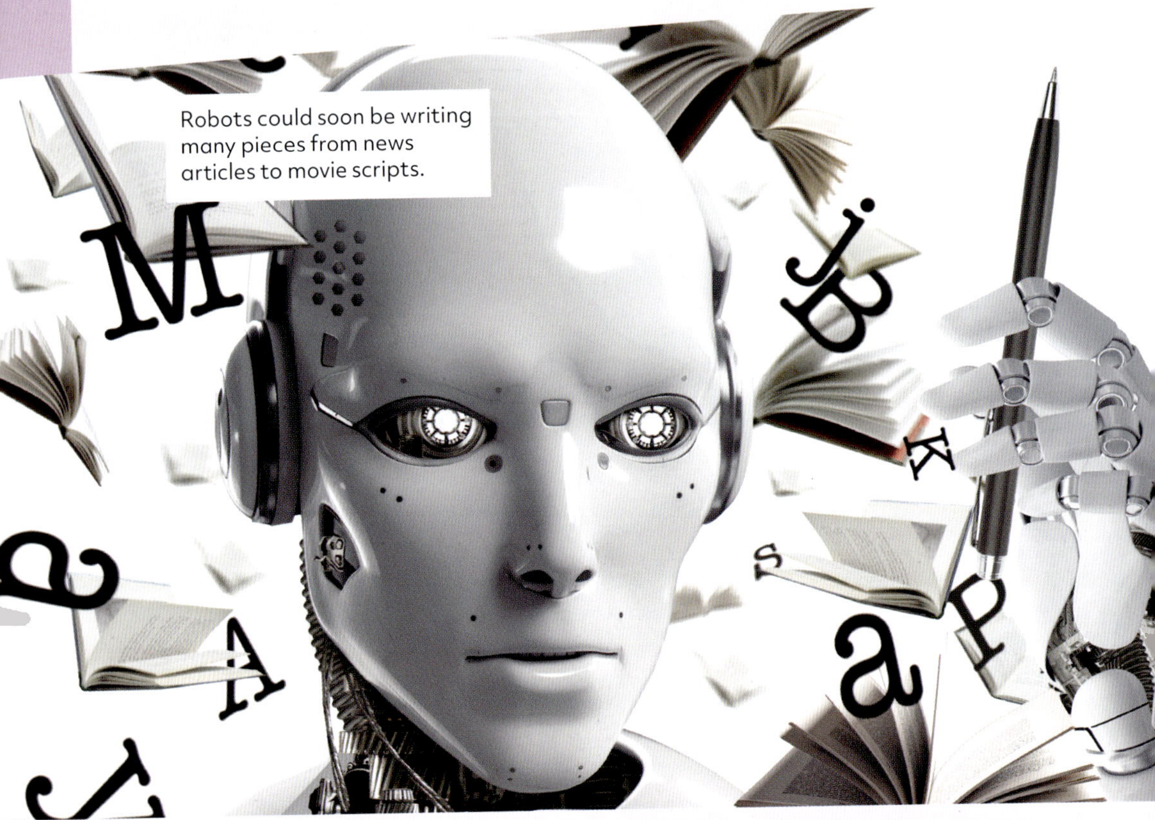

Robots could soon be writing many pieces from news articles to movie scripts.

MEDIA AND MARKETING

The writing may be on the wall for writers. Generative AI systems can generate text and designs for brochures and websites that market products. There are predictions that most news articles will soon be written by AI. While AI may not have the creativity to create the next Harry Potter or write an amazing original screenplay, AI is very good at writing variations of things that already exist. Maybe the AI will not produce the same quality as a human writer, but it's good enough, quicker, and cheaper too.

LEGAL WORK

Lawyers are highly skilled and are well paid to advise on the details of the law and to draw up contracts for individuals and businesses. However, AI tools can create complex legal documents very quickly, as most contracts are based on rules and agreements that already exist. This could well mean that the world needs fewer lawyers. Legal advice is very expensive, which can exclude low-income people from getting the best advice. Use of AI lawyers could lower costs and enable many people to get access to the legal advice that they need.

TRANSPORTATION

Millions of people are employed in moving goods and passengers from one place to another, from

Writers in Hollywood have taken strike action to protest the impact of AI on their work.

cab drivers to the crews of vast container ships. Use of AI in self-driving vehicles could mean that there are fewer jobs in these areas. Self-driving trucks can travel long distances to deliver the goods we need without stopping to rest. They would deliver goods faster and cheaper than any human.

Skilled jobs such as firefighting are unlikely to be impacted by AI, although autonomous robots could reach locations that are too dangerous for humans.

WHICH JOBS ARE SAFE FROM AI?

Around one-quarter of jobs are likely to have little or no exposure to AI. These include skilled physical jobs such as firefighters, people who work in childcare, barbers, and hairdressers. The activities these people do cannot be easily replicated by AI or autonomous robots. Most manufacturing and factory jobs are unlikely to be directly affected by AI.

Many factories have replaced people with machines, such as use of robots on an automobile production line. However, these robots are usually designed and programmed to perform clear specific, repeated tasks rather than to "think" and plan as an AI robot would be expected to do.

CREATING NEW JOBS

The AI revolution will also create new jobs and industries, just as changing technology often has done in the past. This is more difficult to predict than the effects on current jobs. For example, before the growth of the Internet, most people would not have foreseen the huge growth in roles focused on social media, from marketing products to online influencers. We can already see that skills in working with AI are becoming more important to many employers as they begin to search for their next generation of workers. There are also likely to be more jobs created that involve understanding and working with complex data.

THE LIMITS OF WORKPLACE AI

However, just because AI can do a job, it does not mean that it will be used for that purpose. One survey carried out in 2016 looked at how jobs have changed in the United States since 1950. They found only one job that had almost completely disappeared —elevator operator. Other jobs may have been changed by computers but they still exist.

In many industries, humans will be able to do the jobs more effectively than an AI system, and people like to deal with people. Most of us would rather learn from a human teacher, for example.

BIG ISSUES

Sometimes there are legal or **ethical** reasons why a job needs to be performed by a human. For example, if an AI robot prepares a prescription for some medication incorrectly and causes harm to the patient, who is responsible for that? AI will certainly be very useful in the complex work of designing new buildings, but somewhere along the line, a human architect needs to be responsible for the results. This is especially true if something goes wrong with the building. It will never be enough to say that the computer just made a mistake—a human must be held accountable.

Would you be happy to have a drone walk your dog or would you rather have a human do it?

Many of us will have to compete with robots for jobs, as well as competing with other people.

RICH AND POOR

Even if AI may not replace entire industries overnight, there are good reasons to think that AI tools could lead to a more unequal distribution of wealth. Business owners will be able to increase their wealth by use of AI. This is especially true for large technology corporations such as Amazon or social media businesses, which will be able to gain all the benefits of AI across their millions or even billions of customers. While the owners and **stockholders** of these businesses get richer, they will provide jobs for fewer people as AI tools can easily manage online contact with customers and others.

HOW TO COMPETE?

AI could also reduce earnings for many workers. In the 2000s, a corporation might employ people in less wealthy countries to make their products or answer customer questions. They would pay these people less than similar workers would earn in North America or Europe. In the future, competition may not be between workers in different parts of the world but between workers and AI tools that work quickly, don't need to sleep, and never want to take a vacation!

BIG DECISIONS

Ideas about what could happen to jobs in the future usually assume that people will still be taking decisions about who to hire and how to use AI. However, AI tools will have a growing role in business planning. In the future, AI could play a major part in making decisions for a business. AI is able to plan based on data and decisions made in the past, but will these decisions be in the interests of human workers?

Experts agree that governments and other people in authority will need to take action to support workers dealing with changes because of AI. This could mean helping workers adapt to new ways of working or **retraining** for new jobs. People in developing countries are likely to be vulnerable to these changes as they may feel the negative effects of AI, without benefiting from the positive aspects of AI in the workplace. They will be less able to retrain to adapt to the ever-changing workplace, and it may be these people who suffer the most losses because of the new technology.

See pages 26-27 for more on the debate about AI and job loss.

What Is Universal Basic Income?

Some people have suggested the idea of a Universal Basic Income (UBI) to support people who are affected by the AI transition. Unlike welfare payments, the government would give money to all adults, whether they are working or not. This will provide for basic needs of all citizens if whole industries are taken over by AI. Some people think this may be the only fair way to plan for AI. Others think that it would be unfair to more heavily tax successful people and encourage other people not to work.

Small business owners may lose out because they cannot afford to use AI technology.

The Debate:
AI Will Lead to Mass Unemployment

Many people are very concerned that AI will lead to mass unemployment and this could have a major impact on how our societies work. There are arguments both for and against this scenario. Let's take a look at some of them.

AGREE

AI will impact many industries: AI will affect more job sectors and industries than have been affected by previous change, and in a very short time, which will mean that jobs will be lost faster than people can adjust and retrain for new industries.

Incentives for employers to use AI: Many employers will see big advantages in using AI for greater efficiency and cost savings. Businesses that spend too much on human workers may be at a disadvantage because they will not be able to compete.

Adoption of AI is good for all: Some people argue that we should introduce AI as widely as possible because it will make goods and services less expensive or even free to users. They argue that if AI creates mass unemployment, this will be less of an issue if money is not as important to people as it currently is.

DISAGREE

AI will create jobs: Just like every past change in technology, AI will lead to the creation of new jobs and industries that don't yet exist. These will include AI specialists but also jobs that may not involve directly working with AI. That will benefit many people.

Most AI tools will perform specific tasks: There are many examples of tasks that AI can do for humans, but many of these tools will be designed to do specific tasks, such as analyzing data and creating reports, so they will not replace the adaptability of human workers.

No one wants AI to take all jobs: AI can only achieve the objectives set by humans. There are many good reasons why corporations value human workers and customers prefer to interact with humans, so this will limit where AI is used. People will have a place in the workforce.

Conclusion

Most experts agree that AI will cause jobs to be lost in some areas. New jobs will be created but it is unlikely they will replace all the jobs that are lost in the short term. However, AI is already common in areas such as customer services and has changed people's jobs but mass unemployment is not yet a big problem in most societies as a result.

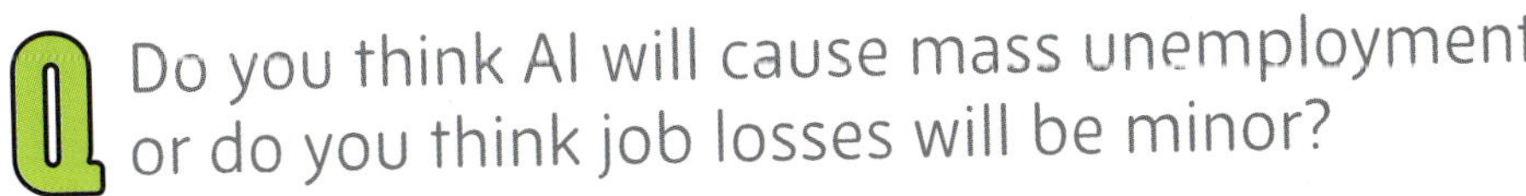

Q Do you think AI will cause mass unemployment or do you think job losses will be minor?

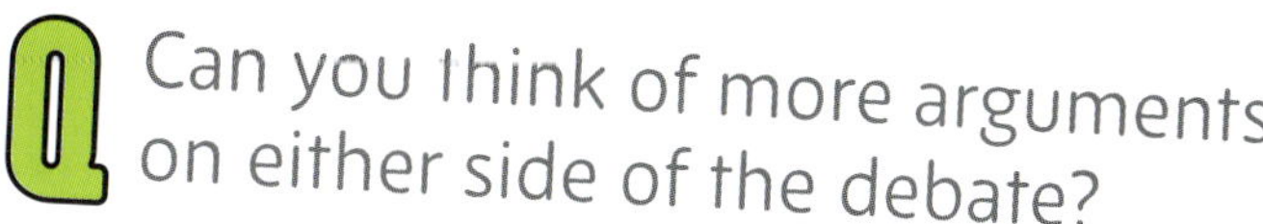

Q Can you think of more arguments on either side of the debate?

Q Will AI be a friend or a foe? What conclusions do you draw?

CHAPTER 4

Cybercrime and Security

One part of the economy in which thousands of jobs have been created in recent decades has been dealing with **cybercrime** and Internet security. Cybercriminals are people who try to commit crimes on the Internet. Those crimes range from stealing money to circulating harmful information or **malware**. With the huge rise in cybercrime, Internet security has become a big concern for businesses.

COST OF CYBERCRIME

In 2025, it has been estimated that damage from cybercrime will cost companies and individuals more than $10 trillion. Companies often hold databases of customer details such as passwords and credit card information that can be extremely valuable to **hackers**. Cybercriminals could be operating from any part of the world, so there is little that national police forces can do to combat them. The huge damage done by cybercrime gives companies a big reason to try and find AI solutions to the problem.

PART OF THE PROBLEM

Unfortunately, AI can be helpful to both sides in this huge online battle. Cybercriminals can use AI technology themselves to create new malware and computer viruses. More complex **phishing** attacks and scams that can use AI tools that have mastered natural language or **cloned** information make them even more difficult to detect. Most worryingly, AI can create many variations of these threats at high speed to try and evade, or hide from, security software. Once attacks are launched, they can continually update with little effort from the cybercriminals. AI works at such speed that it can crack strong passwords much more quickly than in the past.

CREATING FAKE INFORMATION

Generative AI tools can create all sorts of **deepfake** information, including fake photos, to steal someone's identity and use this online. Deepfakes are difficult to distinguish from the real thing and, sometimes, telling the difference is impossible. The use of deepfakes could help cybercriminals steal money or commit fraud.

Creating images using AI will enable cybercriminals to make fake identities more convincing.

CYBERCRIME BONANZA

Experts believe that AI has created a whole range of new opportunities for cybercriminals. Businesses will find it difficult to keep up with the level of threats they face. This could lead to an AI "arms race" as security experts try to stay ahead of the criminals in this online war.

COUNTING THE COST

Cybercrime has costs for all of us. Better security powered by AI will mean extra work for businesses, and, unfortunately, the cost of this will be passed on to **consumers**.

Machine Learning

Machine learning is a term that describes how AI systems are trained to look out for particular types of information, such as words, lines of code, or other patterns. Powerful computers can scan data quickly to spot patterns that they have come across before. This function of AI systems enables them to detect patterns in data that could be viruses or malware, so the systems can deal with these dangerous threats.

CYBERCRIME SOLUTIONS

The use of AI security tools will enable businesses to be constantly scanning for threats and the search for malware will be able to delve deeper than ever before. AI systems will spot suspicious patterns or users that are very difficult to detect with current software. They can then make predictions about what will happen, based on similar events. Finally, AI can take action to prevent attacks, such as disabling accounts, preventing loss of data, and keeping business owners informed about threats.

FIGHTING CRIME WITH AI

Police departments and other security services can also be helped by developments in AI. Much of their work in catching criminals involves looking at data from phone records, social media messages, and analyzing CCTV cameras. Identifying a suspect from hours of video footage can be difficult and time consuming. However, AI facial recognition tools can instantly identify faces that match images on a database. AI systems may also be able to analyze crime data to predict where and when crimes are most likely to take place.

AI can analyze data from CCTV much more quickly than a human.

Facial recognition can help police identify criminals, but could also be used to spy on us.

DISCRIMINATION AND BIAS

One of the benefits of AI systems is that they should be able to make decisions based on evidence rather than the **bias** and **prejudices** that affect many human decisions. However, this has not always been the case and this is concerning if use of AI becomes widespread.

LEARNED BIAS

There have been cases where police were accused of unfair treatment of certain groups of people. If AI is using past crime data to predict where crimes are most likely to take place, there is a risk it will repeat any bias in the existing data. For example, AI systems have been used to decide on sentencing for criminals and when they should be released from prison. A study of one of these systems found that Black people were unfairly being **categorized** as being higher risk than other groups.

PRIVACY ISSUES

One of the biggest issues with the use of AI in fighting online and offline crime is that this conflicts with our right to privacy. Today, many public places are covered by security cameras to prevent crimes. AI facial recognition software may be able to identify criminals, but it can also identify anyone else if it has the data to recognize them. Can we be sure how this information will be used? For example, some governments use data about their citizens to identify anyone who says or does anything that criticizes the authorities. Could data gathered by AI be used by authorities around the world to control people?

Even if our government is not using AI to identify people who disagree with it, right of privacy is important and we should be able to trust that **regulations** will protect our rights as AI systems continue to develop.

The Debate:

AI Will Help Fight Cybercrime

Cybercrime is a big issue for all of us and we need to ensure we do everything we can to safeguard our devices and our personal information. Perhaps AI will help us in the fight against cybercrime. There are arguments both for and against this scenario. Let's take a look at some of them.

AGREE

Speeding up detection: Machine learning will enable AI systems to spot online threats more quickly than ever before. The ability to find patterns in data and software is one of the key benefits of AI.

Dealing with threats: AI systems will be able to make decisions about how to detect malware and develop software to fix bugs or weaknesses in software that might enable criminals to access data.

Covering gaps in the workforce: Online security is a fast-growing industry that needs workers with a lot of specialist knowledge. There are not enough trained people to deal with the threats to corporations. AI can help to fill some of these gaps.

DISAGREE

More threats than ever before: AI may be part of the solution but it is also a big part of the problem. Cybercriminals can use AI to create fast-changing online threats so there is a risk that the situation is getting worse rather than better because of criminal access to AI systems.

AI can be tricked: AI systems are not perfect and are only as good as the data they have been trained on. Sophisticated cyberattacks may be able to trick our defensive AI systems and stay one step ahead of them.

AI protection costs money: While governments and big business will be able to pay for complex AI tools to protect their systems, small businesses and individuals will not be able to do so. That makes it likely that malware will spread via the weakest links in a network.

The risk of human error: Many online crimes and scams rely on people clicking on links that will cause their computers to be affected, thereby being tricked into supplying their own data to criminals or not ensuring that their devices are protected. AI will help to warn people about this but human errors will always happen despite the protection of AI systems.

Conclusion

Experts are most worried about how cybercriminals will be able to use AI to commit crimes and they may get ahead of those who are trying to protect us. However, it is certain that AI will have a big part to play in protecting us all from cybercrime in the future.

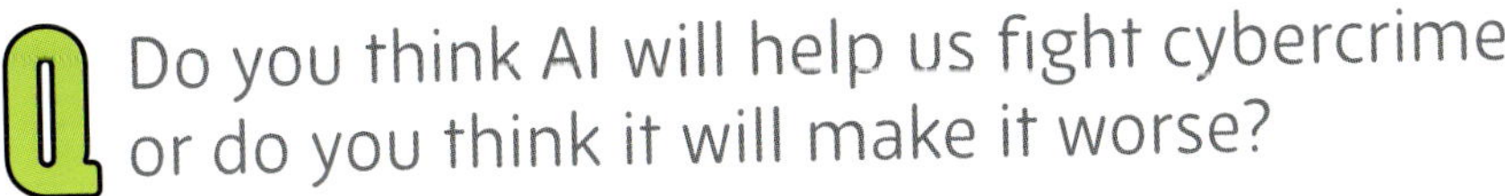

Do you think AI will help us fight cybercrime or do you think it will make it worse?

Can you think of more arguments on either side of the debate?

Will AI be a friend or a foe? What conclusions do you draw?

CHAPTER 5

Are You Ready for AI?

The growth of AI in the workplace is likely to affect all of us in one way or another, whether it becomes part of our working lives or the way we communicate with businesses and other organizations. It may also influence the career you choose, whether you want to work with AI technology or if you don't want to work in a job that may be canceled out by AI in future.

FUTURE SKILLS

We have already seen many ways in which AI will change the world of work. Many routine tasks and jobs that previously required a college degree may be taken over by AI. New skills will be in demand that cannot easily be replicated by AI. While AI tools may be able to create something in the style of a brilliant artist or composer, AI is a long way from creating truly original art or design. The ability to communicate and influence other people will also be highly valued as AI has a lot to learn to truly understand how to communicate and empathize with different people like a human can.

We also know that AI will change some jobs and industries faster than ever before. Many jobs that are common now may disappear. This means that workers will need to be adaptable and open to new technologies in the workplace like never before. We will all have to be flexible and ready to change.

Original art uses skills that are difficult for AI to replicate.

AI can help in making music, but human creativity is also essential.

HIRED BY AI

AI technology is already part of the process of applying, recruiting, and selecting people for many jobs. A lot of job applications are now completed using generative AI tools to create resumes and application letters. Job applications often include tests and assessments, and studies have shown that AI can perform better than most humans on these assessments.

INTERVIEWS WITH AI

For companies, hiring new employees costs a lot of time and money. Recruiters must read applications from large numbers of candidates and then spend time interviewing them. AI can automate this lengthy process either by checking applications or finding ideal candidates based on online profiles. It can even conduct interviews with the candidates.

Human bias can affect who is chosen for a job. AI could make recruiting fairer.

FAIRER RECRUITMENT?

In the traditional recruiting process, only a few candidates may be selected for interviews. Ideally the choice is based on the candidate's experience and how they would do the job. However, there are plenty of examples of bias and discrimination in recruiting. Recruiters might be more likely to favor someone based on how they look, where they went to college, or another factor.

REMOVING BIAS

By contrast, AI interviewers would be able to give hundreds or even thousands of candidates the same interview process, with candidates being successful based only on how they answer the questions and the information on their applications.

For many people AI would make recruitment much fairer because it would remove the chance of bias and discrimination. However, there have been a number of examples of biased results from AI systems. For example, if an industry or job is typically done by women rather than men, this key data could be reinforced by the AI system, making it more likely to recruit women.

PRIVATE INFORMATION

AI recruiters will also be able to access a huge amount of other data about job applicants. Even those who are using the AI tools probably don't have a detailed idea of the very complex algorithms and training that the system uses to make decisions. When making or recommending a decision, the AI tool could be drawing on all sorts of private information such as social media posts or bank details. Unless we understand how the AI works, it is difficult to put safeguards in place to fully protect people.

WATCHING THE WORKPLACE

The influence of AI on the workplace will not stop once an employee is hired. Companies are keen to monitor how their employees are working. This is especially true if they are working from home or at **remote** offices. Many companies already monitor how much time their employees spend on computers or when they are sending messages.

This may be about keeping an eye on employees' health as well as checking up on them at work.

WATCHED AND WORKING AROUND THE CLOCK

AI could make the **surveillance** of employees much more detailed and could extend to their lives outside work. Many experts warn that it is very important to set up safeguards to protect workers' right to privacy. Others point out that workers will be unhappy about too much surveillance and could move to work somewhere else. This is one of many issues that AI could raise in the workplaces of the near future.

Will people be happy about the way AI changes their work lives?

The Debate:

AI Will Take Control of Businesses

The biggest risk that many people see with AI is that computers could become so intelligent and powerful that they could eventually escape human control and start to make decisions that would be negative for people and the way we work. There are arguments both for and against this scenario. Let's take a look at some of them.

AGREE

Human success relies on intelligence: Humans are able to shape the world because of our intelligence. Other animals may be faster or stronger. If AI is able to achieve human-level intelligence, or even improve on it, it will be able to make decisions without human involvement. That is dangerous.

AI computers already have some advantages: AI systems can already process data and make decisions much faster than humans can, so they already have an advantage if they can match human intelligence. That makes us vulnerable.

We need to plan for the future: Most experts think that Artificial General Intelligence (AGI), which are AI systems that can think like humans, is a long way away. However, we need to plan now if we are to stop computers becoming too powerful in the future.

DISAGREE

AGI is not in our near future: Most experts think that the AGI that could change the balance between humans and computers is still a long way off in the distant future. AI systems will still be limited to specific functions and domains for some time to come.

AI has to be designed by humans: At the moment, AI needs humans to design and train the systems. Even quite minor changes to tasks or the environment in which the system works can mean that AI needs to be redesigned by people.

AI is a distraction from other risks: While it is possible that AI could become superintelligent in the future, there are many other risks we face before then that are more important to deal with, such as climate change. AI can help us be more efficient and fight those very real risks.

Conclusion

AI is currently a long way from the point at which computers and robots could take over from humans. While AI can use data to make decisions, there is still a lot of work to do before AI robots can move and think in the same way as humans. However, AI does come with risks that will have to be overcome by us.

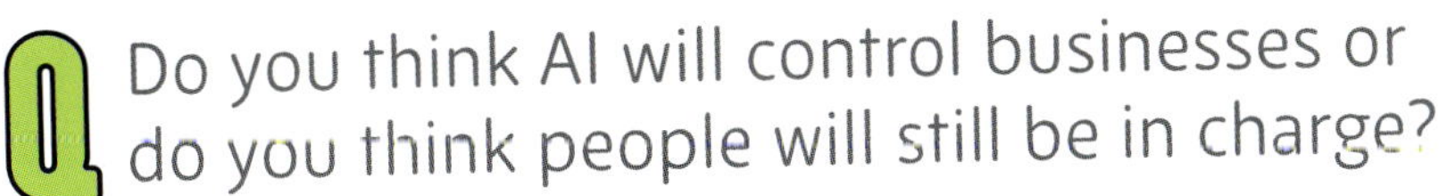
Do you think AI will control businesses or do you think people will still be in charge?

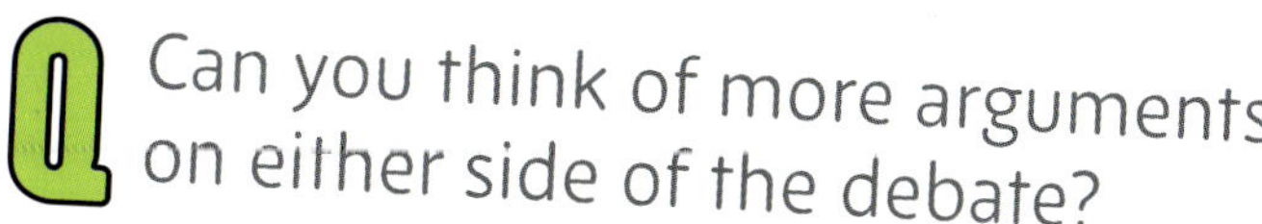
Can you think of more arguments on either side of the debate?

Will AI be a friend or a foe? What conclusions do you draw?

CHAPTER 6

Friend or Foe?

The many uses for AI in industry and the workplace are already changing the jobs of millions of people. AI technology is developing so quickly that the changes this will bring soon are difficult to predict. In the long term, AI could usher in a very different world of work. People are excited about the benefits of AI but cautious about some of the possible negative effects on our lives. There will be winners and losers from the AI revolution.

WHO WILL BE THE WINNERS?

Consumers will benefit because AI will make communicating with businesses more efficient in the long run and will hopefully make many goods and services less expensive because businesses will employ fewer people.

Businesses will benefit from AI, which will make processes more efficient. AI's ability to classify and make decisions based on data will also help businesses to know much more about their customers.

One far-less-welcome group of winners from AI could also be the cybercriminals who try and trick people into revealing passwords or stealing their money. AI will give them powerful new ways to trick and mislead people. Hopefully, more effective AI tools will also help us in catching these cybercriminals.

WHO WILL BE THE LOSERS?

The losers of the AI revolution at work will be working in the industries where AI has the most impact, such as customer services, administration, and transportation. Many jobs will be replaced by AI. New jobs may make up for some of the effects of AI, but these will need people with knowledge and experience of AI technology.

If AI technology does lead to mass unemployment, this will be very difficult for people to deal with. Governments will have to look at solutions to make sure this does not lead to huge social problems.

Another group of losers could be small businesses that are unable to invest in AI in the same way as their bigger competitors. Businesses in developing countries could be at a great disadvantage unless the benefits of AI are shared equally.

AI can bring benefits to all of us, but there are also risks. What if AI becomes too powerful and starts to make decisions that humans believe are wrong? People may end up working in corporations that are effectively managed by machines.

The prospect of AI having so much influence on our working lives also raises lots of questions about privacy. In an AI-controlled world, we may not have any choice about sharing our data and our right to privacy might be greatly affected.

Knowledge of how to work with AI will be important for many workers in a number of fields.

The Debate:

AI Will Make Work Better for Us All

Experts predict that the growth of AI will have as great an impact on work as the Industrial Revolution of the 1700s. It will change where we work and what we do. Perhaps AI will improve the working lives of most people. There are arguments both for and against this scenario. Let's take a look.

AGREE

AI will affect every job: While some industries will be completely changed by AI, it is safe to say that all jobs will be affected in some ways. AI tools using data will make better-informed decisions than humans so this should lead to companies making more money. New jobs will also be created.

Reducing routine tasks: Many office workers feel they spend too much time on routine tasks such as writing emails or scheduling meetings. AI will be able to take over many of those things and do them much more efficiently. Human workers will be able to concentrate on more interesting things.

Speeding up new ideas: Use of AI should create environments in which new ideas can be designed and created more quickly, which will make work more rewarding. That will be a benefit to workers everywhere.

Making work safer: As well as routine tasks, AI robots may be able to take over tasks that are dirty and dangerous, such as working underwater or going into burning buildings so firefighters don't have to.

DISAGREE

Job losses: There is no doubt that AI will take over some jobs, so people will have to adapt to major changes or unemployment. At least in the short term, these changes will be negative for many workers.

Benefits of AI will go to the richest: The benefits from AI will not be equally distributed. Tech billionaires are investing huge sums into AI because they expect these investments to make them even richer. Poorer countries may not benefit from AI at all. That's not fair.

Surveillance at work and privacy issues: AI will give companies and managers more opportunities to snoop on what we do at work and outside work, affecting our right to privacy. People may have the choice of being managed by a machine or simply replaced by one!

Conclusion

There will be benefits of AI for many people, but there will also be costs such as job losses in some industries. We must hope that companies and governments work together to harness the benefits of AI and reduce some of the negative effects on ordinary people.

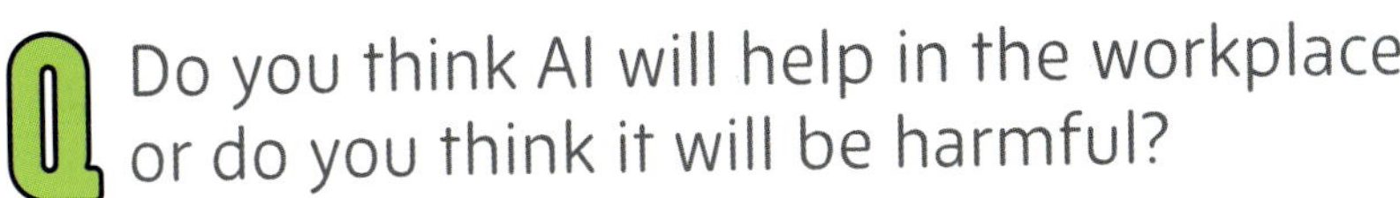

Q Do you think AI will help in the workplace or do you think it will be harmful?

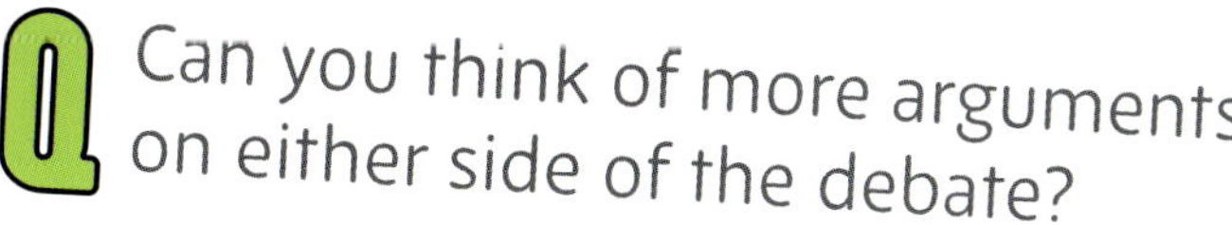

Q Can you think of more arguments on either side of the debate?

Q Will AI be a friend or a foe? What conclusions do you draw?

The Ethics of AI

To ensure that people enjoy the benefits that AI can create around the world, developers and governments need to think carefully about how AI will evolve. The below rules will need to be considered.

- Respecting rights: This includes the right to privacy, but also the right not to face discrimination and to be treated fairly.
- Being transparent: Workers need to know when AI is being used to make decisions, such as when hiring employees or changing business processes.
- Accountable and fair: Being accountable means that humans check decisions made by AI. AI tools may treat everyone the same, but this does not mean that they are being fair. Humans ought to be involved in deciding if something is fair.
- Promoting safety: Computers may be able to work all the time but people can't. AI needs to ensure that workplaces are safe.

Some people question whether AI will make the world more or less equal. This could cause arguments and disputes between different groups of people and nations. International regulations will need to address some of these concerns.

Q Would you add anything to this list?

Q What rules would you put in place to ensure that AI will benefit the widest number of people?

Find Out More

BOOKS

Alicia Z. Klepeis. *Artificial Intelligence and Work: 4D An Augmented Reading Experience* (World of Artificial Intelligence 4D). Capstone Press, 2019.

DK. *Simply Artificial Intelligence* (DK Simply). Dorling Kindersley, 2023.

McPherson, Stephanie Sammartino. *Artificial Intelligence: Building Smarter Machines.* 21st Century Books, 2019.

Miller, Michael. *Cyberspies: Inside the World of Hacking, Online Privacy, and Cyberterrorism.* 21st Century Books, 2021.

ONLINE

Discover how generative AI could change hiring as we know it:
www.bbc.com/worklife/article/20230419-chatgpt-how-generative-ai-could-change-hiring-as-we-know-it

Find out more about how AI could change the future of work at:
www.cnbc.com/2023/04/28/how-ai-could-change-the-future-of-work.html

Listen to Google's developers speak about the future of AI:
https://youtu.be/880TBXMuzmk

Find out more about how AI systems learn at:
https://youtu.be/R9OHn5ZF4Uo

To find out more about AI you can also search for websites of companies involved in AI such as OpenAI, the creator of ChatGPT, and Google's DeepMind.

Publisher's note to educators and parents:
All the websites featured above have been carefully reviewed to ensure that they are suitable for students. However, many websites change often, and we cannot guarantee that a site's future contents will continue to meet our high standards of educational value. Please be advised that students should be closely monitored whenever they access the Internet.

Glossary

algorithms processes or sets of rules to be followed for a computer to solve a problem or perform a task

artificial describes something made by humans and not naturally occurring

automated operated without human control

avatars computer-generated images of people, such as used in a game or online communication

bias being in favor of one argument or group of people, which may be unfair to others

categorized put into a category, or type or group

chatbot computer software designed to communicate with human users online

classify to give something a class, or say it is in a particular group

cloned made an exact copy

consumers people who buy and use something

currencies systems of money, for example, the US dollar is a currency

cybercrime crime committed using computers and the Internet

database a system of information

debate an argument or discussion about a particular subject, in which arguments are given for and against the main question

deepfake a form of AI that uses deep learning to create fake images

deep learning a method of artificial learning that teaches computers to process information in a similar way to the human brain

dictate to speak to another in order for them to record what you are saying

drones powered aircraft without human pilots on board

ethical relating to moral rules that decide how people behave

foe an enemy

fraud criminal deception for financial or personal gain

hackers people who break into computer systems

hardware the wiring and other physical parts of a computer system

malware software that is designed to disrupt or damage a computer system

natural language processing (NLP) a type of machine learning that enables computers to understand and communicate with natural language

navigate to determine a location and plan directions, or find the way around a system

pesticides chemicals used to kill pests that harm crops, such as insects

phishing fraudulently sending emails or other messages for financial or personal gain

pioneer the first person to do something

predict to say what will happen in the future

predictions ideas about what will happen in the future

prejudices bias or discrimination against people or things

productive getting a lot done quickly

regulations rules or laws

remote far away from a main building, such as a company's office building

replicate to copy or reproduce

retail the selling of goods to consumers

retraining reprogramming someone and training them again

robot a machine that is able to replicate human functions or movements automatically

routine an organized and known order by which things are done

software programs or instructions that affect how a computer operates

stockholders people who own or keep hold of stock, or things that can be sold

surveillance carefully watching and monitoring something

transcribing writing or typing heard words

Index

advertising 8, 12, 13
algorithms 7, 36
avatars 13

banking and finance 9, 20, 27
bias 31, 36

chatbots 4, 8, 13, 19
ChatGPT 11
concerns about privacy 31, 26, 27, 41,
    41, 44
concerns about security 28, 29, 30,
    31, 32
corporations 8, 15, 16, 24, 26, 32, 41
costs and saving money 14, 17, 19, 21,
    26, 33, 35, 43
creating fakes 28, 29
cybercriminals 28, 29, 30, 32, 33, 40

debates 5, 16–17, 26–27, 32–33,
    38–39, 42–43
deep learning 9
discrimination 31, 36, 44

factories and warehouses 8, 9, 19, 22
farming 14

Google 7, 11
governments 25, 31, 33, 40, 43, 44

jobs and job losses 5, 9, 10, 14, 18, 19,
    20, 22, 23, 24, 25, 26, 27, 28, 34, 35,
    36, 40, 42, 43

legal work 21, 23

machine learning 29, 32
making decisions 4, 24, 31, 32, 36,
    38, 39, 40, 41, 42, 44
making mistakes 12, 15, 23
media and marketing 4, 8, 10, 21, 23,
    24, 30, 37
Microsoft 11

offices 6, 10, 11, 14, 15, 37, 42

productivity 10, 14

robots 9, 19, 20, 22, 23, 24, 38, 39, 42

software 4, 11, 12, 28, 30, 31, 32

transportation 21, 40
Turing, Alan 7

About the Author

Nick Hunter is a highly experienced children's book author, who has written countless titles on many subjects, from history and science through social studies and geography. In writing this book he has discovered that AI is an incredibly powerful technology that has the potential to bring great benefits to the workplace if we manage its potential risks.